#POST

THIS

BOOK

DAViD SiNDEN & NiKALAS CATLOW

sourcebooks
fire

Copyright © 2015 by David Sinden and Nikalas Catlow
Cover and internal design © 2016 by Sourcebooks, Inc.
Text and illustrations © 2015 David Sinden and Nikalas Catlow

Sourcebooks and the colophon are registered trademarks of Sourcebooks, Inc.

Published by Sourcebooks Fire, an imprint of Sourcebooks, Inc.
P.O. Box 4410, Naperville, Illinois 60567-4410
(630) 961-3900
Fax: (630) 961-2168
www.sourcebooks.com

Originally published as Post This in 2015 in the United Kingdom by Macmillan
Children's Books, an imprint of Pan Macmillan.

Library of Congress Cataloging-in-Publication data is on file with the publisher.

Printed and bound in the United States of America.
VP 10 9 8 7 6 5 4 3 2 1

Also by David Sinden &and Nikalas Catlow

Anti Journal

You can share photos and videos online instantly and they can be a really great way to connect with friends and let the world know what you're doing. But it's worth remembering it can be difficult and often impossible to delete pictures or videos from the Internet entirely. Once you share something online, you lose control of it—it can be copied and shared further. And you're sharing it with more than just your friends. Anyone and everyone can see it. Think twice before posting something you might later regret.

This book will spark your creativity
and fill your social media feed
with creative, fun images.

Respond to its prompts in any way
you wish, whether on or off its pages:
by filming, photographing,
drawing, or making.

Express yourself without need for
perfection and post all images with
the hashtag #PostThisBook

Explore the hashtag to see how others
use this book to spark their creativity.

Capture yourself holding
this book for the first
time, before life changes.

 Take a photo

and POST it
with the hashtag #POST THIS BOOK

I AM HERE

#PostThisBook

Point this arrow. Take a selfie of where you are now. POST IT.

Complete and share this: #POST THIS BOOK

"Me in 3 words"

- - - - - - - - - - - - - - -

- - - - - - - - - - - - - - -

- - - - - - - - - - - - - - -

Fill this square in any way you like

#POST THIS BOOK Square compare

Attempt to draw a
PIG IN A WIG #POST THIS BOOK

Post a photograph
that plays with light #POST THIS BOOK

Create
outside
this book.

Paint an egg.

Share it #POST THIS BOOK

Take a 360-
degree video

#PostThisBook

Grow this seed **#POST THIS BOOK**

WHAM BAM KERPOW!

Express yourself as if
you lived in a comic

#POST
THIS
BOOK

Tag a friend

Respond to each of the prompts below. Create on the pages of this book or outside it using any medium you like.

LINES

ADD EYES TO ANY OBJECT

A view through a cardboard tube

#POST THIS BOOK

AN IMAGE INSPIRED BY GOOGLING THE WORD STRIPES

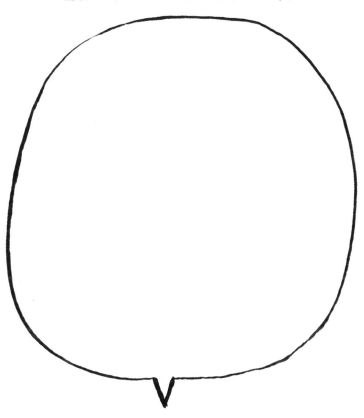

 Make him shout

IN MY DREAMS

📷 POINT

CHILLING

HEALTHY!

& SNAP #POST THIS BOOK

TICKETS

FILM THIS FILLING UP

#POST THIS BOOK

#POST THIS BOOK MUG SHOT

📷 Customize then hold
   your personal mug

While creating with this book, treat every in-between or leftover space as a canvas, however small.
Doodle, pattern, and color around things. Fill up the background.
#EverySpaceUsed

Film fast food

▶

#POST THIS BOOK

or food going fast

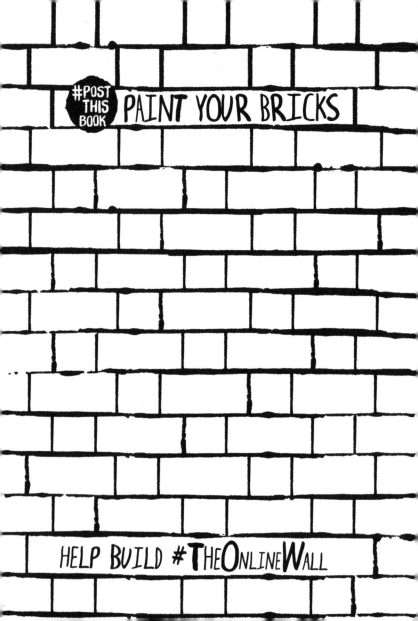

Decorate stones

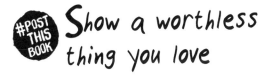

Show a worthless thing you love

GRAVITY IN ACTION

Decorate
a branch

Hat on
a pet

WHAT DOES A SNIGLET LOOK LIKE?

Rehome this penguin in the outside world. Photograph it in its new habitat.

#POST THIS BOOK

(UpdateYourPage)

Make a new profile pic

#POST THIS BOOK

#POST THIS BOOK

Turn this
WILD

#POST
THIS
BOOK

Post found
numbers
#LookForNumbers

Create a foot
monster

Add another cat
to the Internet

AND OFF THE PAGE

#POST THIS BOOK

📷 Point and snap

BESTIES

#POST THIS BOOK

Express any of these:

TOPPLE! SPIN! JUMP!

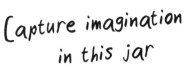

Capture imagination in this jar

#POST THIS BOOK

 #POST THIS BOOK Open the jar

Point your camera upward.
Find art in the sky.

POINT AND SNAP

Point your camera downward.
Find art on the ground.

Decorate and share on a Monday #PostThisBook

Show the adventures of a toy

Rearrange flowers

Bling

 Overlap shapes

USE A NEW
APP OR EFFECT
e.g. levitation, panorama,
pop art, slo-mo,
superimpose

#POST
THIS
BOOK

Create using bits and bobs
#POST THIS BOOK

Depict a song without using words

#POST THIS BOOK

GUESS MY SONG

#POST
THIS
BOOK

Whirl your colors

HANDMADE

POINT AND SNAP

Retail therapy

Add real
fabric to
this bag

#POST
THIS
BOOK

Show something
out of place

Turn anything into a unicorn
#SeeTheUnicorns

FROM A BUG'S POINT OF VIEW

#POST THIS BOOK

Film

a journey in

time-lapse

Celebrate a celebrity

POST THIS TO REACH THE CELEBRITY

An image inspired by #POST THIS BOOK googling the word PATTERN

CREATE A PATCHWORK
#TheMassiveBlanket

#POST
THIS
BOOK

#POST THIS BOOK

Expand and color

NAIL ART

#POST
THIS
BOOK

↑
Your hand here

Be misguided
with makeup

FILM a THUMB WAR
in costume

A thing in multiple

#POST
THIS
BOOK

ADD AN ABSTRACT EXPRESSION

#POST THIS BOOK

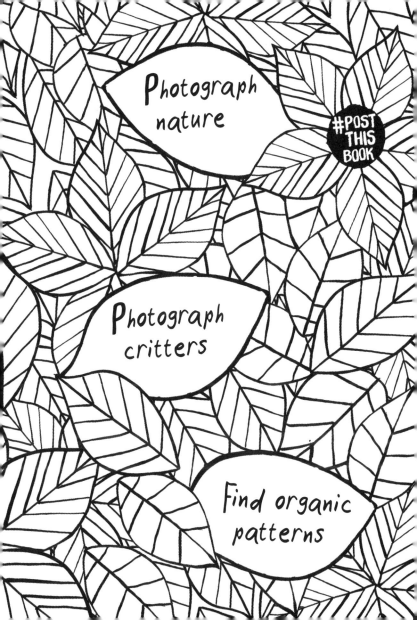

Photograph nature

#POST THIS BOOK

Photograph critters

Find organic patterns

Depict yourself as an animal

#POST THIS BOOK

FILM IN REVERSE
#PostThisBook

LET LOOSE
HERE
#POST
THIS
BOOK

CREATE A SCULPTURE OF
YOURSELF USING A POTATO
AS A STARTING POINT

#POST THIS BOOK

#POST
THIS
BOOK

Display your materials

FAKE A *TATTOO* YOU'D REGRET

Show lines on your hand

An Image from My Generation

 Who remembers this?

Color a storm

#POST
THIS
BOOK.

CAKE FACE

POINT
AND SNAP

DANCING FEET

Share a four-word poem

I award you this for AWESOMENESS

#POST THIS BOOK

Post this to praise someone

Attempt a balancing act
#POST THIS BOOK

Create from any online tutorial
#PostThisBook

Draw on a photograph
#PostThisBook

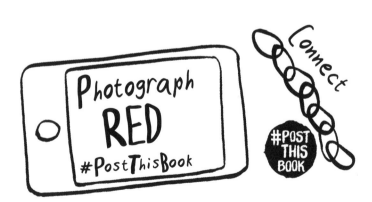
Photograph RED
#PostThisBook

Connect
#POST THIS BOOK

#POST THIS BOOK

Freeze-frame a game

#POST THIS BOOK

BUBBLES

Make a piece of toast your canvas

GROTESQUE PORTRAIT

INCOMING!

#POST THIS BOOK

POINT & SNAP

#POST THIS BOOK Fingerprint folk

#POST THIS BOOK HOW MY BRAIN WORKS . . .

YiPPEE it's FRIDAY

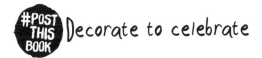

#POST THIS BOOK Decorate to celebrate

#POST THIS BOOK Expand and color

Blooming colors

Show the breeze

Mummified selfie

REPEAT
REPEAT
REPEAT

Ooze happiness

#POST
THIS
BOOK

What's he looking at?

Take a photo portrait of someone without showing their face

#PostThisBook

STYLE THIS PAGE

#POST THIS BOOK

Keep something in here

Film one action. LOOP IT

#PostThisBook

Me when I looked different

#POST
THIS
BOOK

My #PostThisBook
workspace

📷 Point and snap

TANGLE THIS PAGE #POST THIS BOOK

#POST THIS BOOK EXPAND and color

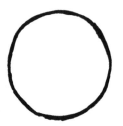

Capture the effects of rain

#POST THIS BOOK

Utilize a plastic bottle

#POST THIS BOOK

#POST THIS BOOK

Take your camera for a walk

Add
color
to a
T-shirt

Add speech
bubbles to
an image

MOSAIC FROM FRAGMENTS

#POST THIS BOOK

OR

#POST
THIS
BOOK

Divide this page #POST THIS BOOK

 Film water

POUT

📷 POINT

YUMMY!

SHOE SHOT

& SNAP #POST THIS BOOK

LIKE

Do your hair differently

Ballpoint pen on a banana

Add flowers here.
Post this, tagging
a friend who
deserves flowers.

#POST
THIS
BOOK

Capture
something
beautiful

MY FACE
AS A
CANVAS

Over-decorate
a cupcake

#POST
THIS
BOOK

Find love for your pet at

#PetLoveMatch

PET'S DATING PROFILE

#POST THIS BOOK

Depict a fictional character from a game, book, or cartoon

LOOK!

IT'S A MEME

#POST THIS BOOK

Animate an
inanimate object

#PostThisBook

The same but different

#POST THIS BOOK

Photograph a souvenir

#PostThisBook

Google the word "art." Share a screenshot.

CREDIT THE SOURCE

#POST THIS BOOK

 #POST THIS BOOK Photograph someone taking a photo

Show a Rapid Recipe

#POST THIS BOOK

#POST
THIS
BOOK

RESPOND ON

Covered in spots

PAPER-BAG
HEAD

BUTTONS

AND OFF **T**HE PAGE

MEMORIES
#PostThisBook

POINT
AND SNAP

TOTES CUTE!
#PostThisBook

USE THIS PAGE TO CONTINUE
ANOTHER PICTURE #POST THIS BOOK

THE OOPS! PAGE #POST THIS BOOK

1. Finish your life's **To** Do list
2.

Remove your shoes

Record a day in snippets

#POST THIS BOOK

#POST THIS BOOK Gummy Bear Horror Show

EXPLODE
COLOR

Record laughter

 Present food
artistically

FIND A FACE IN AN **O**BJECT

#POST
THIS
BOOK

Color this in

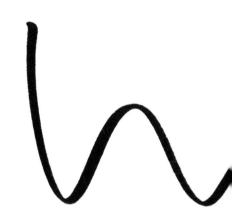

#POST THIS BOOK Show the death of a tomato

#POST THIS BOOK FILM A PART OF YOUR ROUTINE

EXPAND AND COLOR

Create
an outfit by
positioning

clothes on
the floor

#PostThisBook

#POST
THIS
BOOK

Completely
cover an
object in color

Fake an antique photo

RECORD PIECES OF A PLACE

POINT AND SNAP

WALLPAPER

THIS

ROOM

#POST THIS BOOK

STRIKE A POSE

#POST THIS BOOK

Odd socks

#POST THIS BOOK

Point and snap 📷

#POST
THIS
BOOK

SHOW A
COLLECTION

Turn a
thing SCARY

Refashion
fashion

#POST
THIS
BOOK

#POST THIS BOOK Finish THE FACE

Express any of these: ▶ //

SPLAT! BURST! WOBBLE!

IMITATE SOMEONE ELSE'S WORK THAT YOU LIKE

#POST
THIS
BOOK

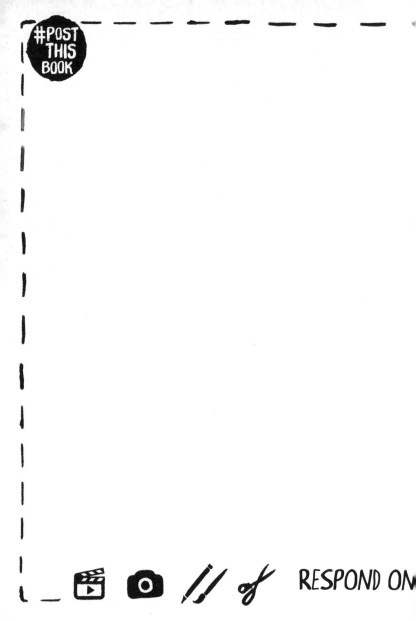

RESPOND ON

Beach art

Yesterday's technology

PRESS
YOUR
FACE

AND OFF **T**HE PAGE

Stick-man tragedy #POST THIS BOOK

#POST THIS BOOK

Model a surrealist's hat

Take an abstract photograph

Test color combinations

Start Here.
Go beyond the
edges of the
book

#POST
THIS
BOOK

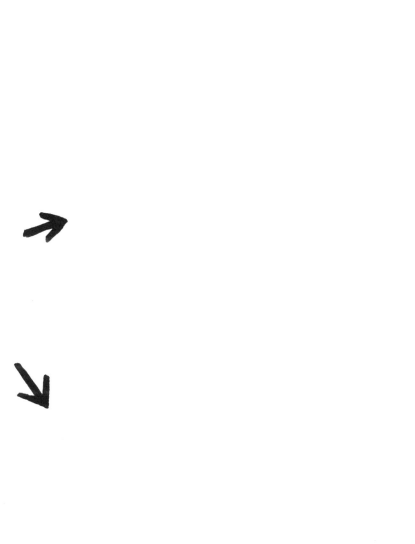

#POST
THIS
BOOK

MESS WITH
THE SCALE
OF **T**HINGS

Use a window
as a frame

Create a ghostly effect

Devise a tabletop obstacle course **#POST THIS BOOK**

#POST THIS BOOK Photograph reflections

#POST THIS BOOK Attempt a tricky throw. Record it.

 Photograph a secluded spot **#POST THIS BOOK**

 Time-lapse a TIDY UP **#POST THIS BOOK**

RESPOND ON

A close-up
view

Paint a leaf

RECORD A
BUILDING

#POST
THIS
BOOK

AN IMAGE INSPIRED BY
GOOGLING THE WORD
COLOR

#POST
THIS
BOOK

Film
a silent
scream

#POST THIS BOOK

The first item
I'd save from
a fire

Point and snap

Build a badly made model
#POST THIS BOOK

Capture
SHADOWS
#POST THIS BOOK

FILM AN
ANIMAL
#PostThisBook

Use a boot
as a vase
#POST THIS BOOK

Zombify **#POST THIS BOOK**
something unlikely

#POST
THIS
BOOK